DAUREL AND BETON

DAUREL AND BETON

A twelfth-century adventure story

translated by

Janet Shirley

Llanerch Publishers, Felinfach

ISBN 1 86143 040 X

CONTENTS

Introduction

The story of *Daurel and Beton* is interesting, unusual and important, but first and foremost it is entertaining. The characters and the story grip the reader - in its own time will have gripped the audience - and we race on, thinking, 'How could he do such a thing?', 'He can't mean that!' or 'But heavens, why didn't she - ?' Part of our amazement is due to the conflict between twelfth-century assumptions and ours, assumptions that we may not even know we have. We are sure we know the difference between right and wrong, and so were men and women then, but our basic truths can be very different from theirs. Inherited status, rank, did matter profoundly. Women, poor things, did in Bible truth need to be guided and controlled by men. Practical considerations did demand the immediate remarriage of a widowed woman who held a great fief. Loyalty, love and tenderness, however, were virtues then, as now. The past is only partly a foreign country.

It is not possible to discuss these questions in detail without giving away the story and spoiling it for readers. The text is what matters and people will want to have their own response to it. For this reason I shall not put forward any discussion of the themes of the text, important though these are. They include the status accorded to women, the care of infants and children, teenage love, the supposed genetic transmission of character traits and the sworn comradeship of warriors. This comradeship was a well known feature of a life mainly devoted to warfare - if ever you needed to be able to trust the man at your back, it was in the mêlée of combat - but the length to which Duke Bevis takes it can only amaze modern readers. There is no apparent implication of any homosexual affection. The tie between lord and vassal is drawn with equal vigour, and the extreme sacrifice Daurel and his wife make to save the life of their infant lord is presented as unquestionably heroic. The role of the Church in that 'age of faith' is also interesting: bishops and archbishops are often referred to, but marriages and even baptisms seem to be briskly conducted with no need for a priest. Music and the entertainment arts figure largely. The Islamic world appears as a refuge full of courtesy, kindness and delight.

With that proviso, we can get down to facts. *Lo romans de Daurel e de Beton* was written by an unknown author, probably in the late twelfth century, almost certainly in the Poitou region of what is now France. His language was a form of Occitan, not French, although he sprinkled his text with fashionable French words. Both Daurel and Beton in different ways are heroes of the story, Daurel as a minstrel who displays true nobility and Beton as a baby at risk whom Daürel rescues. The picture of the infancy of this child is one of the most unusual features of the text. He is a happy baby, who wins people's hearts by smiling at them, but the portrait is sketched in securely with a few key phrases, and never becomes sugary.

The manuscript

The text exists only in a single manuscript: Bibliothèque nationale, nouv. acq. franc. 4232, which Kimmel says is by several hands, none of them good. It has been damaged by damp and by worm-holes, so that there are a number of gaps and disputed readings. The end of the story is missing, and although it is possible to invent a happy ending which rounds off the tale as we have it - a laughing Charlemagne might welcome his nephew's courage and seek reconciliation - it is more likely that a large part of the text is lost, and that the story went on to tell of Beton's heroic revolt against imperial oppression. This would bring it into the 'rebel barons' cycle, linking it with such works as *Girart de Roussillon* and *Raoul de Cambrai.*

Versification

The text as it stands consists of 52 rhymed *laisses* or sections of varying length, mainly but not entirely written in ten-syllable lines; a few are alexandrines. The *laisses* do not work as units as they do in the older epics, but are merely gatherings of lines rhymed together. The text does have structure and movement, but this comes from the shape of the overall narrative and the brief recapitulation passages, not from the nature of the *laisses.* The *laisses* are numbered 1 - 52 for ease of reference to Kimmel's edition of the text.

Date

Kimmel maintains that this version of *Daurel e Beton* was written after 1170, and that it is based on an earlier poem composed between 1130 and 1170. Charmaine Lee places its composition later, at the turn of the twelfth and thirteenth centuries. See the bibliography for both these authorities.

Location and place names

The language and the rhymes used point clearly to an author and a setting located in the south-west of France. So does the frequent mention of Poitiers and of the church of St Hilary there. This is not the main church of Poitiers but one that lay near the west boundary of the medieval town, near a gate through which pilgrims would pass on their way to Santiago de Compostela. Kimmel remarks that the name of the ill-used lady, Esmengart, may echo that of a ninth-century queen of France, Ermengarde, who was a benefactor of St Hilary's.

Poitiers and Paris have a very real ring, and do indeed lie three days' hard riding apart (334 km) as suggested in section 51. (It is interesting that Charlemagne holds court in Paris, not at Aix-les-Bains, as he did in historic fact and in earlier epic tales.) Antona and Montclar, however, could be anywhere, and all we are told is that they are not far from the sea. If we accept the suggestion put forward by Charmaine Lee as to the interpretation of *on sol esta lo leo* in section 21, this is likely to be the Atlantic coast - which may go some way to explain why it took Beton three months to sail there with fair winds from 'Babylon'; that is, from Cairo and its port, Alexandria. Dolphins are mentioned too, and a fisherman and 'great waves'; the sea is important in this story.

The Ardennes is a traditionally dark and dangerous forest, and according to both Meyer and Kimmel could be found anywhere in France, not necessarily in the north west. 'Dark Valley' too (*Brunas Vals*) is a typically epic place of danger.

Charmaine Lee, however, places the Ardennes forest in its true geographical location, links Antona with Southampton and suggests a northern influence on the poem, even including Hamlet-like themes. As she points out, the poem comes from Poitou, where there was certainly 'an Anglo-Norman presence'. She draws attention too to the contrast between *Brunas Vals* and Montclar, 'bright mountain'. She also recalls an historical ruler of Provence and Lombardy, who was crowned king in 879. His name was Boson or Beuson and he married a lady called Ermengarda.

Some difficulties of translation

The text uses titles oftener than names - 'the great duke', 'the noble lady', and so on. This can sound stilted in English, so I have occasionally used names where the text does not. Names of people and of places are also sometimes used for the sake of clarity where the original has pronouns - not, 'he went there', but, 'Bevis went to Antona'.

'Love' is always a difficult word to translate. Two separate Latin words, *amare* and *aestimare*, lie behind *amar* (French: *aimer*), so that what looks like, 'I do not love you' probably means, 'I don't think much of you'. When Charlemagne or Count Guy declare an intention of loving someone, it means that they propose to behave towards that person in a fair and generous manner. Liking or loving does not come into it.

Another awkward word is the noun or adjective *pros* (in French, *preux*). It includes a range of meanings. Cotgrave's Dictionary gives: "Hardie, doughtie, valiant, coragious, full of prowesse; also, loyall, faithfull, sincere, honest, vertuous, worthie; also, discreet, skilfull, readie. *Les neuf preux.* The nine Worthies." 'Worthy' is not a word to excite admiration nowadays, and I have used various terms - 'good, valiant, brave' and so on. It is an epithet frequently used of Daurel the minstrel, of Esmengart the great lady, and especially of Beton in section 41, where Daurel tests the boy's courage and then assures him that if he lives he can be sure he will be a *pros.*

Select bibliography

Daurel e Beton ed. Paul Meyer, Paris 1880.

A Critical Edition of the Old Provençal Epic 'Daurel e Beton' A.S.Kimmel, Chapel Hill (University of North Carolina) 1971.

Daurel e Beton a cura di Charmaine Lee. Parallel texts in Provençal and Italian, Parma 1991.

References to the wealth of articles on this text will be found in the bibliographies of Kimmel and Lee.

Acknowledgements

Thanks are due to many helpers, but principally to Dr Linda M.Paterson, who first suggested putting this text into English and has kindly supplied reprints and references. I should also like to thank the Librarian and staff of the Taylor Institute in Oxford for their prompt and unfailing assistance.

This is the story of Daurel and Beton

1

Would you like to hear a fine song?

Listen! I'll tell you about a great duke of France, about Count Guy, about Daurel the minstrel, and Beton, the boy who suffered so much as a child.

High on a dais sat Bevis, duke of Antona, his Frenchmen all around him, great nobles every one of them. Count Guy - God give him sorrow! - was among those present. Guy had nothing, no town, no fief, nothing but a single castle, Aspremont.

Duke Bevis took him by the hand and said,

'Guy, you are nobly born, you are my vassal, and poor. And you are my liege man, I know that for a fact.'

'I can't contradict you, my lord,' said Guy. 'All this is true.'

'Count Guy, I grant you my whole fief. * Let all men hear it!' he cried aloud. 'You shall be lord of my house just as

* This translation follows Meyer and Kimmel, who emend the text *lo menague* to read *lo meu alue*, 'my allod'. A different version would follow Lee, who interprets *menague* as 'ménage', and translates '*la cura dei mie beni*', 'the care of my goods'.

much as I am myself. Now, swear comradeship to me for the rest of our lives! If I take a wife but have no children, and I die before you do, then, comrade, she is yours. My castles, towns, fief and household, good comrade, I give to you, I put them wholly at your disposal.'

'A princely gift, my lord!' said Count Guy. 'As this is what you want, I accept. Paid so handsomely, I'll lead your armies and risk my life wherever in the world you command.'

'We'll swear to it,' said Duke Bevis. He sent for a book of the gospels and on it they swore comradeship and then kissed each other on the chin. Sworn comrades, one true, one false!

2

Duke Bevis took this oath in his palace at Antona before five hundred witnesses. A faithful friend and a traitor!

For ten years the two men lived in harmony, sharing their fiefs and forces, until one day God sent great preferment to Bevis. He was standing in his palace with some of his leading men, judging a plea, when up galloped a messenger from Charlemagne. The messenger dismounted, went forward and greeted the duke politely, then took his hand and drew him aside to speak:

'I'm sent to you by Charles, king of France. You must go to him, and take your friends with you, for he has a scheme in mind which will make you all rich.'

'Certainly I'll go to him,' replied Duke Bevis, 'and I will take my brave comrade Guy.' (How well the duke trusted him, how disastrous this was!) 'To you, friend,' he said, 'I shall give my handsome palfrey and my swift charger. Go to the king - God keep him from harm! - and tell him I shall join him before the month is out.'

'My lord,' said the messenger, 'I shall be happy to obey you, and I am most grateful for your gift and your welcome.'

3

Charles' messenger set off, and Duke Bevis ordered one of his runners:

'Quick, go to Aspremont, tell my comrade Guy to come and see me.'

'Gladly, my lord,' said the messenger.

He reached Aspremont and there under an olive tree found Guy - liar, traitor! - playing backgammon. Guy looked at him.

'My lord,' said the runner, 'may I speak with you? The duke has sent me to Aspremont because you have business at Antona.'

'Saddle my charger,' Count Guy said to Bertrand, his squire. 'We'll go and ask the duke what he wants.'

Cheerfully they got ready, and rode to the high palace at Antona. When he saw Guy, Bevis went forward and embraced him, saying,

'God keep you, my friend and true comrade! Charlemagne has sent for me, and I am going to take you to Paris with me to pay court to the emperor.'

'My lord,' said the count, 'as you wish, so be it!'

Duke Bevis was ready to leave for court, taking with him an escort of two thousand knights. Great duke as he was, he felt pleased to be summoned by the king. Just as he was about to ride off, a minstrel came in, took out his viol and played a merry, pleasant and lively tune. He had few possessions, this minstrel, but admirable manners.

'Friend, what's your name?' asked the great duke. 'Don't conceal it!'

'I am Daurel, my lord,' answered the minstrel, who knew how to make the best of any situation. 'I am a fine harpist, I play the viol, and compose excellent poetry. And I am your vassal, my lord, from a strong castle called Montclar.'

'In that case, friend, I must take good care of you,' said the duke. 'You shall come to court with me.'

'My lord,' said Daurel. 'I cannot do that. My wife and two sons depend on me, and I have no silver or gold to leave with them.'

Duke Bevis sent for Azemar, his seneschal.

'Friend,' said the duke, 'by the faith you owe me, protect this man's wife for him, dress her richly, and look after the two children. Give them from me everything they can ask for, whatever it costs, wherever in the world you can find it.'

'My lord,' said Sir Azemar, 'God bring you safe home! They shall lack nothing that I can provide for them.'

'Daurel,' said the duke, 'take this white palfrey to ride, it should carry you well.'

Speechless with joy, Daurel stooped to the duke's shoe and tried to kiss his foot, but the duke lifted him up, and he had him handsomely fitted out.

'My lord,' said Guy, 'we should not be dawdling! Dear friend, duke and comrade, let's use our spurs!'

They gathered up their reins, rode off and reached Paris on a Saturday evening.

4

On Sunday morning at daybreak Duke Bevis and Guy got dressed. They both wore tunics of good Tyrian silk. The duke made Daurel go with them; he went to court to play his viol and dance. When the emperor of France saw the duke approaching, he rose from his seat and went forward to welcome him, took his hand and made him sit down beside him. He put an arm round his shoulders and said,

'Duke, you don't know why I sent for you, but you'll know soon, before we let you go. Before you leave, I shall ask you ...' *

'Sire,' said the duke, 'I am most grateful! You only need to give me orders, but you are also pleased to give delight!'

But Count Guy heard this exchange and said to himself:

'Comrade, for this woman's sake, you'll die!'

5

Great was the court in France, great the gathering in the high palace before Duke Bevis of Antona and the emperor! Dukes and counts filled the halls, heroes and warriors were there, bishops and archbishops and all the flower of knighthood! Duke Roland himself was present, as were all the Twelve Peers, mighty and valiant.

Then Charles the Great said,

'Listen to me, my lords! Bring me my noble sister! With your approval, I shall give her in love to a husband, to Bevis the great duke. I shall also give him Poitiers, all its buildings and towers, and will make him lord of Bordeaux.'

* Some words are lost here. Guy's comment below shows that Charlemagne is offering Bevis his sister Esmengart in marriage.

But Guy, felon and traitor, muttered,

'This woman will bring him to a painful death!'

6

'Up sir!' cried Charlemagne the proud. 'My lord Count Oliver, on your feet, and fetch me my charming sister!' Very gladly he brought her, a delightful girl, lovely to look at, fresh as a rose in bloom. The king stood up and spoke to Bevis:

'Duke of an ancient house, son of my dear friend Ogier, stand up and take my noble sister to wife!'

'A gift not to be refused!' exclaimed the duke. The king took her and handed her to the archbishop, who made her kiss Bevis three times. There in the high palace the wedding was celebrated. If only you had been there, what rejoicing you would have seen!

And Guy, the lying traitor, said,

'Comrade, you'll suffer for this woman's sake!'

'Listen, my lord duke!' said Charles, giver of light. 'I grant you my standard to bear and my great host to lead and command.' Duke Bevis kissed the king's hand and as standard-bearer accepted his glove.

The duke remained at court a full month, and then he and Guy went together to King Charles.

'King and emperor, I have a request to make on Guy's behalf: if you love me, I ask you to hold him dear.'

'I shall make him my counsellor,' said the king, 'and for your sake he shall be dear to me.' Then the great duke kissed him, took leave and he and his wife left Paris. And Daurel played tunes on his viol and rejoiced because the king of France had given him a warhorse. Away rode Duke Bevis, happy and contented.

Guy the traitor - may Jesus spurn him! - coveted the duke's wife Esmengart.

7

Away rode Bevis the great duke very cheerfully towards Poitiers, and with him went Lady Esmengart, all smiles and laughter. She rode a fast palfrey, its saddle ivory, the poitrel silver. Two thousand valiant knights formed their escort.

False-hearted Guy spoke pleasantly to the duke:

'Comrade,' he said, 'I'll tell you what I want - how lovely my lady is, so beautifully made! Will you give me my share, as we agreed?' Laughing, not seeing any treachery, the brave duke replied,

'Comrade, ask the Almighty Father to kill me off quickly, and then, as you like her, she shall be yours!' Between his teeth the traitor answered,

'I shall kill you with my shining spear!'

On they rode till they could see the high towers of the strong city and the citizens coming out to welcome them, some five thousand people, all dressed in their best. Joyfully they rode onto the stone paving, where the town and its government were handed over.*

And the noble duke accepted all the fortified places and granted the revenues to the miscreant traitor, Guy! The whole extent of the fief, all Bordeaux and its appurtenances as far as Agen, all was put under his control.

8

The great duke summoned his court. Daurel's wife came forward; Daurel played the viol and she danced and tumbled before the lady; they gave a charming performance. The duke was very pleased to see them all so happy and said to his lady,

'What an admirable pair!' Then: 'Daurel, I am going to give you a strong castle called Montclar. It's on the coast

* This translation of *Redon la viala e l'ausor mandamen* follows Meyer. Kimmel takes *viala* to mean 'victuals' and suggests that the citizens welcomed their lord with banquets and handed over the fortress. Lee has 'cedono la città e la rocca.'

not far away; its harbour will make you rich. * All who live there are to be at your command. Go, you and your wife, make your home there; I grant it you for your lifetime, and you may bequeath it as you wish after your death.' And Duke Bevis had the castle granted and made over to Daurel - that was a well contented minstrel!

Count Guy - God never help him! - was scheming to amass silver and gold. But what Duke Bevis longed for was to carry the emperor's standard. Whenever Charles rode out to war, he sent for the duke, who went to assist him.

One day the duke had gone hawking along the riverbank and Count Guy wanted to speak to him. He did not find him, but Lady Esmengart happened to come by. Knowing that her husband loved the count and liked to do him honour, she welcomed him kindly. He took her hand and they sat down together on a bench to talk.

'Lady,' he said, 'I can hide it no longer - I love you! Be kind, I beg you! Love me, let me be yours. Come to bed with me, don't make me wait!'

'Scoundrel!' cried the lady. 'How dare you think of such a thing? The duke loves you, loves you dearly, and you want

* Or, following Meyer, 'and the port is well situated.'

to deceive him! No one in the world can trust you, not if you are trying to dishonour Duke Bevis!'

'Lady,' said Guy, 'perhaps you love him too much! By the Lord who hung on the cross, within these two months you'll be my wife, for I am going to kill him, he cannot escape me.'

'Wretch!' she exclaimed. 'God loathe and detest you! Your words will disgrace you, I shall see to that!'

Then Guy went away, having no inclination to linger.

Noble Duke Bevis came back from hawking and went to put his falcon on its perch. When he came in, the meal was ready and he washed his hands and sat down.

Lady Esmengart wept bitterly, and the duke saw this and stopped eating. Half out of his mind with anxiety, he exclaimed,

'Lady, how unhappy you are! Who has annoyed you or upset you? Is it because you had to leave France, your own country? My sweet lady, do you want to go back there?'

'That never crossed my mind,' said the lady. 'I'll tell you later, when they've taken the table away.'

After dinner she went and put her arms round him.

'Oh, my lord duke, this is what I've got to tell you - that wicked Guy - Jesus hate him! - came in not long ago, and finding me alone, he spoke to me, and wanted to dishonour me! I answered angrily and he threatened me, said he would kill you, you couldn't escape him, he would destroy our love.'

'Lady,' said the duke, 'don't be angry! He only said that to test you, to see if anyone could tempt you. There's not a man in the world I rate so highly!'

Oh God, how can the noble duke trust him as he does? And Guy did indeed kill him when they went hunting together.

9

God gave a child to Bevis the great duke. Rich and poor, high and low, all were delighted. Bevis sent the baby to Roland's palace, to be joyfully baptised there. Roland had him baptised with splendour, for he was his kinsman, and gave him as good a name as he knew, Beton. Beton, what a name of suffering that was to be! Roland sent the child back to the duke in a silver cradle, with an escort of a thousand valiant knights. They were welcomed home with joy; great was the duke's happiness, great the thanks he gave to God.

The child was well cared for, but only for a single year. After that trouble came when Duke Bevis went hunting in the great Ardennes forest.

Duke Bevis was sitting on a bench beside Lady Esmengart, his wise and brave wife, when a messenger came running up.

'My lord,' he said, 'listen! There is an enormous wild boar loose in the Ardennes, they're hunting it everywhere, especially in the oak woods.* I have never seen an animal like it, never!'

'I shall go after it!' said the duke. 'We'll hunt it down and make a present of it to my lady and little Beton. I'll take my brave comrade Guy with me.'

Hearing this, Esmengart was very upset. She wrenched her glove between her hands, ripped it in two and exclaimed,

'Oh, my lord duke, why do you trust him? He has never loved you and never will. He intends to kill you, you'll be at his mercy!'

'Lady,' said Bevis, 'say whatever you like! I'll never suffer any harm or distress if Guy can help it, not as long as I live.'

'Oh God,' said the lady, 'what nonsense I'm hearing! I know he will break my heart.'

The great duke ordered one of his messengers:

'Go and fetch me Guy from Aspremont castle.' Off he went at once, fast and cheerfully.

* *Pertot lo.s cas e dabant tot l'aglan*, an obscure line. I take *aglan* to mean 'acorn', and thus by extension 'oak trees'.

10

Along the highway came the traitor Guy, riding fast and planning his crime. He would kill the duke while they were out hunting. Now he entered the palace where Beton lived. Bevis saw him and said,

'Comrade, we are going after a wild boar, a big one, very strong, and we shall bring it down!'

'Excellent, my lord!' answered Guy. 'It won't be too strong for us. We'll bring it home and give it to Beton.'

Noble Esmengart heard this from her own room, wrung her hands and tore her furred gown, called to the duke and kissed him on the chin.

'My dear love, Jesus keep you! Don't trust that traitor Guy! It was a bad day when he became your comrade! It's dangerous to trust him, he'll kill you, you'll be quite helpless!'

'Lady,' said Bevis, 'this really is nonsense! You and I will quarrel over it.'

'Go then!' said Esmengart. 'As it's what you wish, go with him, and God's blessing go with you!'

11

'My lord duke,' said Guy, 'let's be moving! Have the hounds and brachets coupled, and we'll only take a few men with us, just four good huntsmen. And you and I, my lord, we'll ride our fast coursers and strike the boar! However strong it is, it shall fall!' The lady listened to these evil words and went into her own room, where she wept bitterly, ripped off her dress-fastenings and tore her furred gown. The duke's men led out his swift courser.

12

Just as the duke was about to mount, Daurel the good minstrel came forward.

'My lord duke,' he said, 'I have great cause for joy - a little son is born to me, and I want to ask you a kindness - would you be pleased, my lord, to baptise him?'

'Go and fetch him,' said the duke. Daurel did so, for he very much wanted this done. He brought the child and presented him to the duke, who named him Daurelet of Montclar. Then the duke mounted and prepared to ride off. His lady came and kissed him - for the last time! - and said,

'God bring you safely back, my lord!'

Valiant Duke Bevis called up the hounds. They found the boar in Dark Valley, but could not get it to move - hounds or no hounds, it would not condescend to get up. The duke had the hounds loosed and the huntsmen blew their horns. Then the boar rose. It scattered the hounds, injured three of them with its great tusks, left the thicket and made for another lair

- this was the Ardennes, a forest no one can measure. *
Now they had to leave the huntsmen behind.

'Let's follow!' Bevis said to Guy.

'We'll bring him down, my lord!' Guy answered.

Spurring with all his might, the brave duke thrust at the boar with such force that he drove his spearhead through its backbone and spilled its entrails out.

'Comrade,' he shouted, 'come and help me! Don't let it get up again!' Guy rode up spurring hard and struck Duke Bevis under the shoulder; he drove the spear right through him and flung him down beside the boar. The duke struggled and tried to get to his feet, but the steel was in his body and he could not stand. On his knees, he cried out,

'Esmengart, lady, what you said was true! If only I had believed you, I should be safe! How kindly you rebuked me, and told me not to love Guy! Ah, my darling, now I understand! Ah, false comrade, what a clever liar you are! You have killed me instead of the boar. False comrade, how could you plan such treachery, how could you do it!'

13

Gravely wounded, noble Duke Bevis said to false Guy,

* This follows Meyer's reading of *adesmar*, an emendation of the ms reading, *adesviar* or *adesniar*. Kimmel emends to *adesar*, 'approach, attain'. Lee translates 'che non si può evitare.'

'Comrade, listen to me for a moment. Be careful, don't pull the spear out until I've told you what to do. I know you'll be accused of my death, but, friend, I'll tell you how to manage: set the boar's tusks in my ribs and drive your spear into the boar. They'll all say it was the boar killed me, no one will contradict you or accuse you. You were my comrade, sworn and pledged. Comrade, I understand why you have killed me - it's because you wanted my wife so much. God help me and forgive me my sins, if only you had told me, I would have given her to you, her and all her great inheritance! I would have gone overseas. For God's sake, don't hurt her! Ask good King Charles to give her to you; he'll do that, you're a man of good reputation, well respected. And little Beton - take care of him, I beg you. Bring him up, count, in your own court; he's Charles' nephew, it'll be no dishonour to you. You shall have half of all he possesses.'

Like a chained lion Guy looked at him; like a winged angel the duke looked back.

'What nonsense you talk!' said false Guy. 'By that same Lord who hung on the cross, the child shan't live another two weeks. If I can get him into my hands, no town or castle shall protect him. You I have killed; he's not done with yet.' The good duke looked at him, and joined his hands as in prayer:

'Comrade, please, bring a leaf, give me communion.'

'In God's name,' said Guy, 'you talk such rubbish! Hurry up and die, you're taking too long. I'll cut the heart out of your body and slice it in two!'

'Nonsense, comrade,' said Bevis. 'You'll be richly avenged for the wrong I have done you. Take out my heart, my lord, taste it! Lord Jesus Christ who hung on the cross, who humbled yourself to be born for our sins, Mary, blessed Lady, hear my prayer - if it be your will, keep my son Beton out of his hands, and forgive me my sins!' And false Guy went up to him, pulled out the spear, and the duke died. The duke is dead, he will not come back.

Now Guy the traitor rammed the spear into the boar and set the boar's tusks in the duke's side. He took his knife and jabbed it repeatedly into the body, as if the boar had been eating it. Then he blew the horn and the huntsmen came hurrying up in alarm. They saw the duke lying wounded and dead, they saw his bloody face and side; of course they were horrified.

'Tell us, Count Guy,' they said at once, 'who killed the duke?'

'It's done me no good!' he said. 'All I know is that I've lost my good lord, my sworn comrade! By the time I reached him the boar had got him down, it had ripped him open and killed him, as you see. How angry I was to see it! I struck at the boar and wounded it, drove my spear right through it and killed it dead. I have avenged the good duke!'

'You villain,' said one of them, 'you have done a terrible thing! You have killed the duke and brought suspicion on us all. No boar ever made that wound, look, it's a palm-breadth across!'

'Friend,' said Guy, 'say what you like! I would never think of such a thing, not for all the wealth God can give! Look at the marks the boar made, and those two tusks there in the duke's side!' The huntsmen did not linger. They laid their lord on four branches and Count Guy, traitor, renegade, laughed in his heart but wept for joy. *

* *Ri ne el cor mas de gauh a ploratz.* Meyer emends *de gauh* to *de fors*, 'outside', giving, 'he laughed to himself but wept outwardly'. This whole section is puzzling. Why does the dying duke try to help his murderer escape punishment? One suggestion is that as the two men are presented as total opposites, one good, one bad, the duke is here shown as a pattern of what a sworn comrade should be, keeping his vow and supporting his fellow in every conceivable situation. Even so, line 433 is difficult, for what wrong does the duke suppose he has done Guy? The ms. reads *del mal que.us fi vos seret be vengatz*, and Lee translates *Sarete vendicato per il male che vi ho fatto* - it really does mean what it seems to. The recommendation to 'eat some of my heart' is equally baffling, and the surely unlikely suggestion has been made that Bevis is anxious to transmit a portion of his own virtuous character to his comrade's evil soul. The duke's request for a leaf is not a problem: in such an emergency a leaf or a blade of grass could be used as a substitute for the consecrated host. Bevis wanted to receive communion before he died.

14

Off galloped Guy the traitor on his bounding courser and outpaced the others. Inside the high palace Esmengart heard the noise of his arrival and ran out. Instantly she was terrified. She saw Guy, glared at him and cried,

'Tell me, Count Guy, how is my lord?'

'Lady,' he said, 'he lies dead in the great wood. The boar has killed him. I am deeply grieved.'

'Lies, you foul wretch! You have killed your true lord! Alas, unhappy that I am, this perjured traitor has robbed me of all my love!' She gave great sighs, mourned and lamented, until with grief, tears and sorrow she collapsed unconscious.

15

Soon the duke's body was brought home and everyone ran to it. What shrieks you would have heard, what faces seen ravaged and hair plucked out! Knights fell senseless, citizens tore their clothes, great ladies lacerated their cheeks till the blood ran. Never has anyone seen such grief!

Lady Esmengart came to her senses and saw Guy standing close beside her. She looked at him and groaned. She could not bear it, but quickly took a knife from a citizen and struck at Guy. It was no use, they held her and would not let go.

'My lords,' she cried, 'listen to me! Just a few days ago he came and threatened me, said he would rob me of my lord, my husband! There he lies dead and my heart will break! Beton is alive, surely he'll avenge him!' She ran to the duke and lifted the pall.

16

'Look there, my lords, see what you think! No boar ever made that wound, it was a spear, by the Lord who gave us speech!' Having said that, she mourned in anguish, tearing her tender flesh. All watched her, and wept. More than ten thousand heard her cry,

'Ah, my lord duke, why wouldn't you take your household troops who guard you so well!'

Daurel the good minstrel now rode up, slipped from his fine dappled charger and collapsed onto the ground, unable to stand. When he came to himself and began to speak, he bitterly reproached Our Lord:

'Ah, Lord God, how could you drive the great duke out of this world? He gave me Montclar castle! I was poor and he made me rich!' He mourned him more bitterly than I can tell you.

Three days they kept him there, then buried him near the altar at St Hilary's.*

* One of the churches in Poitiers; see Introduction page 9.

God keep his soul! Now we will let him be and speak about Guy, may God detest him!

17

As soon as wicked Guy had seen the duke put underground, he went to Aspremont and ordered his chief officials:

'My lords, bring me my treasure.'

'Lord, as you wish,' they answered. They brought it, loaded onto fifteen pack animals.

'Have it all packed up,' he said, 'and go and arm yourselves.'

Three hundred of them rode out well equipped with swords and inlaid hauberks, and Guy, forsworn and faithless, riding at their head. Not till they reached Paris did he stop, and there he went up to Charles's palace. The king saw him, stood up and asked him why he had come:

'How is the duke, my friend and comrade?'

'Bad news, my lord,' said Guy, traitor, renegade. 'The duke, my sworn comrade, is dead. A savage boar, God curse it! ripped open his belly and ribs.' Hearing this, the king was appalled. He struck his hands together and cried out,

'Ill fated!' Great lamentation arose from the whole court and Duke Roland rent his clothes to pieces.

'My lord,' said Guy to the king, 'stop this outcry! If grief could have brought him back, you can be sure ours would have done so. Come this way a moment, let me speak to you.' They sat down on a bench.

'King and emperor, give me a brief hearing. I am told your treasury is much depleted, as you have paid so much out to hired troops. My lord, with your permission, I would like to make up your losses. Look, out there I have fifteen pack-beasts laden with the purest silver and gold. I hold the inheritance,' said the traitor, 'formerly belonging to the duke who has gone from this world. If you see fit, king, grant me these lands. The gold and silver shall be delivered to you at once. Give me the lady, and I shall be your brother-in-law. I shall be a better friend to you than any man born of woman. I am rich; the arrangement will do you honour. I shall take the place of the late duke.'

'That's a fine gift you have brought me,' said the king. 'We will pursue this as soon as we have dined.'

Once the king had this huge sum of money, grief for the duke was quite forgotten. The gold and silver was all stowed away, and the king cried,

'Knights, saddle up!'

He took only a hundred with him, and they rode without pause to Poitiers. One of the knights entered the palace.

'Lady,' he said, 'how are you? Look, here's your brother, come and greet him.' When she heard that, her heart rejoiced.

'Ah God,' she said, 'now I am sure that perjured traitor will die, the brave duke will be avenged!'

Lady Esmengart went down the steps to King Charles and kissed his eyes. But the traitor Guy came up after him and the lady saw him and cried out.

'My lord,' she exclaimed, 'you care very little for me, bringing that traitor with you! He killed the duke! They went out hunting and he drove his spear into his side!'

'Never believe it, my lord!' said Guy. 'She is a lady and may say what she likes. If a man said that to me, I would take my weapons and prove him a liar! The duke was my comrade, pledged and sworn - not for sixty cities could I have planned such a thing!'

'King and emperor,' cried Esmengart, 'I have told you the truth! He killed him, and it's easy to prove. Have a fire lit outside in the courtyard, and I will pass through it, let all the nobles watch me. If one hair of mine catches fire, have me burned, show me no mercy! If God saves me and my truth, let that traitor be dragged by wild horses!'

'Leave off this altercation!' said the king. 'None of it will bring the duke back. You are to have Guy instead of the duke.'

Hearing this, Esmengart cried out,

'Ah my lord king, how easily you decide to give me a traitor instead of the great duke! I think you have been very well paid for this! A noble king indeed, born under a lucky star, who sells his sister for profit! If Beton lives - and he is so little still! - my cause shall be dearly paid for. His father is dead, and now you force me, yes, by the law of force you give me that man as husband. You'll get no thanks from God! Brother,' she begged, 'give me a knight, so that my child is not called a traitor, and my heart will be better contented.'

'You are talking nonsense,' said the king. 'A count is worth more than any lord. I give you Guy, and I require you to accept him.' Then he said, 'Count, marry her at once!'

'Gladly, my lord,' said Guy, 'if it is your pleasure.' The king himself rose to his feet, took her hand and made her kiss him three times.

'Brother,' she said, 'you give me him by force. God who hung on the cross confound you! May lightning strike you before you reach home!' And she took the ring with which she had been married and in the sight of them all threw it into the fire.

18

Great and small, everyone watched her. There was no one there who did not weep for pity; all grieved for her, except the emperor, but they were afraid of him and no one dared speak out. In joy and delight Guy took the lady; in tears and sorrow she took him. The wedding was celebrated in the high palace.

Now good Daurel the minstrel went to her.

'Lady,' he said, 'give me my lord, little Beton. I am afraid that traitor will kill him as he did my lord. I hold Montclar and I will put Beton in the tower there and bring him up in joy and happiness until he reaches his full strength. Once there, he need never fear any count or emperor, no one shall take him from me.' Noble Esmengart feared for her child. Anxiously, quietly, she said to Daurel,

'I have sent him to a sister of mine, she will take care of him for me until he's strong.'

19

The noble lady rose from table and with three countesses went into her bedroom. She struck and beat her face and wrung her hands, exclaiming 'Unhappy!', till blood flowed from her mouth.

'Alas, wretch that I am, born in an evil hour! I loved my husband, I am given to his murderer! Blessed Mary, queen of heaven, advise me, and quickly!'

One of her ladies said to her,

'I can advise you, if you will listen to me: have your little son brought up in secret, so that no one hereabouts knows where he is. When he's fully grown, he'll come, he'll bring knights and very soon he'll win back the fief, he'll avenge you on the man who forced you. On a hill or by the highway he'll have the traitor hanged!'

'That's good advice!' said Lady Esmengart. 'Yes, I like your plan.'

Angry and unhappy, she left her room. The king embraced her and took his leave.

20

The king rode out, taking faithless Guy with him, so that Lady Esmengart was left alone until evening. She sent for a certain man, a citizen who had been a friend of the great duke. He came at once, for he could never fail her.

'My lord,' she said, 'be careful, be kind, and help me, for I'm in desperate need. The good duke who is dead loved you dearly - protect his little son! Look at him here, wrapped in Greek silk. He is your lord, you know that. Help him, and do it quickly! If that foul traitor finds him here, he will kill him, he'll never escape.'

'Lady,' he answered, 'if you approve, I will have him brought up surrounded by the sandy sea. No storms will blow there, there's no cold, no wind, no frost, no evil thing. I will give him an excellent nurse, my own daughter. Her husband is dead and so is their child, whom she never suckled. She shall nurse this baby, as she has none of her own. My older son is brave and courteous, he shall bring them their food and provisions. Nothing evil shall touch him.'

Esmengart thanked him warmly.

'Here, take him then, and be careful of him!'

So the rich citizen took the child out of the bedroom like a thief and quickly got him away to the island. Lady Aicelina was delighted to have the baby to nurse, but she kept him only two months.

21

A house was built for the duke's son, a house which had no internal beams or rafters but stood in the sea among great waves, on a rock where the seals dwell. * A strong gated

* *on sol esta lo leo.* Kimmel emends *leo* to *loc*, 'dwelling', but Lee points out that all the rhymes in this laisse are in -o plus n, which argues for *leo(n).* She suggests 'leone di mare, foca', and adds that this would place the action of the story on the Atlantic coast, probably of Poitou.

wall surrounded it so that no water or storms could enter in. Lady Aicelina - Jesus Christ be kind to her! -kissed the baby tenderly when the time was right, wrapped him in rich silk and then in an ermine gown. Kissing his eyes and his whole face, she sang him a sweet song and begged God to give him a long life.

Thus the child was cared for in secret. The citizen and those of his household brought ample supplies of wine and bread, and the baby slept in bedclothes brought from France. Let us leave him there with God's blessing, and speak of Guy's treachery.

'Lady Esmengart, you have a wicked heart! You have hidden Beton away from me, you are afraid of me, and Jesus help me! I love him just as much as you do. Fetch him here, and we will give him a noble upbringing and then surrender his whole fief to him. The duke was very good to me, and in this way I can repay him.'

The lady stood still and said neither yes nor no. She knew very well there was treachery there.

22

Then she replied,

'Since you ask for him so urgently, you ought to know this - less than a week ago I found Beton dead beside me. He is buried at St Hilary's. If you want him, go and ask for him there.'

'Lady,' he said, 'what a sinner you are, telling such shameless lies!'

'Wicked count,' she said, 'why do you argue? You told me a worse lie, for I know well, better than you would like, that you killed the duke, whom you said you loved. Be sure of this: I shall never be a true wife to you however long you live, for no traitor should be loved.'

This angered Guy; he sprang up, took her by the hair and struck her with the golden spur he had on his heel till the red blood spurted from her sides.

'Murderer!' cried the lady. 'Kill me, I beg you! Beton is alive, that's the real truth, he's being brought up away in France. When he returns, your day will be near! You'll be taken to pieces, torn limb from limb!'

Traitor and renegade, he left the room and summoned two horn-blowers.

'Go,' he told them, 'proclaim all over the fief that if Beton is found, he's to be brought to me at once. Whoever finds him must not delay. I shall pay him a reward of one thousand marks of silver.'

The men proclaimed this in towns and cities as if Beton were a known thief.

Unfortunately it happened one day that a fisherman put out

to sea - Ebrart he was called, forsworn and treacherous! - and chanced to go straight to Beton's refuge. He knocked at the door and went in. Lady Aicelina had Beton in her arms, and he laughed, for he was a happy child.

'God keep you, lady, who are doing such good work and nursing this child like a true woman!'

Kissing his eyes, she greeted him and said,

'Friend, think of God! For the love of God, keep this little child hidden! Be merciful, have pity, for he is your lord, let loyalty win you over! Poor child, he's an orphan, in need of compassion. Look at him, see how he is made, how terrible it would be if he were harmed! How fresh are his mouth and face! He's the duke's son, we know this for certain, it's true. Alas, sir, if you tell the traitor where he is, he will kill him, for he is angry with him. But if the baby lives to grow up, you will be a very great man, for I shall tell him how you found him. It is for you to kill this child or save him!'

'Lady,' he said, 'you are talking nonsense! He's my lord, I shan't be false to him. Be content, lady, take good care of him, live well and cheerfully, for I'll bring you anything you need.' Lady Aicelina raised the child in her arms.

'Ebrart,' she said, 'touch this child! You will be the better for it all your life.' She drew back the silk wrap and the baby smiled at him. 'Look, Ebrart,' she said. 'He's never seen you before and how happy he is!'

'He shall be very dear to me,' said the traitor. Between his teeth the foul villein said, 'One thousand marks of silver I've found at sea today!'

He left them and went hurrying away.

23

This cruel fisherman - Jesus reject him! - did not stop till he found Guy. He arrived just as Guy was about to eat; he looked up and saw Ebrart coming in.

'My lord,' said Ebrart, 'I would like to speak with you. This Beton, how much will you give me for him?' Guy could hardly speak for joy -

'One thousand marks of silver, as I had it proclaimed.'

'My lord,' said he, 'have them guaranteed to me.'

'Friend, I shall be delighted!' said Guy. And then to Daurel, 'Daurel, can I trust you?'

'What a question! My good lord, how can you doubt me? There's not a man in the world so dear to me!'

'Guarantee this man payment of a thousand marks of silver by nightfall, if he can show me where Beton is.'

'I will see that he's paid,' said Daurel.

'I must do this at once,' said Ebrart. 'Follow me to the coast, for that's where I found him when I went fishing. I can show you exactly where he's hidden.'

But brave Daurel ran to saddle his horse and did not stop till he reached the sea, and could get no further.

'Lord Jesus Christ who chose to create me, tell me how I can get there, how I can save my lord from death!'

Now the young man who brought them food came up in his boat, making for the shore. Daurel saw him and shouted,

'Friend, come and speak with me! If you'll put me across, you can ride, I'll give you this dapple grey. Duke Guy wants to kill the duke's son!'

The young man burst into tears, and exclaimed,

'My lord, we must do all we can!' Then Daurel went aboard the boat.

24

They made the crossing with all possible speed.

'How upset you are, my lord!' said Lady Aicelina to Daurel, and, 'Dear brother, why have you brought him here?'

'Sister, you shall know at once.'

'I'll tell you exactly,' said Daurel. 'Guy knows that the duke's son is here, Ebrart the fisherman has sold him. On Guy's instructions I have guaranteed the man a thousand marks of silver. I have prayed to God so hard for this child that in his holy goodness he has led me to him! Lady, I am so glad I have found him! Give him to me, I have been here too long.'

'That's stupid talk, my lord!' she said. 'I shall die with him, that's my destiny.'

All three stood still and looked at the child. Then Daurel went forward, picked him up and fled away like a thief. The two of them crossed over in haste. The lady, most unfortunately, they left behind.

She was tired, and after crying a little she fell asleep, for she had been awake much of the night.

Daurel mounted and rode spurring till the blood ran down his horse's sides. The baby cried and Daurel comforted him, saying,

'Ah, my little lord, how far I've come to find you! Pray God you've found safe harbour!' He did not draw rein till he reached Montclar.

'Ah, Daurel, my lord,' said his gentle wife, 'how exhausted you look!'

'Lady,' he said, 'I was born under a lucky star - I have brought you the duke's son. I found him out at sea, on a island. Look, here he is,' and he put the child in her arms. She held him, sighed, looked up to heaven and earnestly praised God.

'Surely,' she said, 'this was destined! My lord died; we have my lord. He shall be cared for, whoever may be pleased or angry.' She took the baby into the bedroom and satisfied his hunger. Daurel's sons could not have been happier if they had found all the gold in the world. The whole family rejoiced and was glad.

Alas, they forgot the nurse, who was wickedly tormented.

25

Guy the traitor rose hurriedly from table.

'Ebrart,' he said, 'it's time to go!'

'My lord,' said the fisherman, 'there's nothing to wait for.' They shouted,

'To saddle!' and went to arm. Three hundred men went out to hunt the duke's son; many were eager to find him. They rode fast to the coast, found the boat, crossed and reached the child's hiding place.

Now false Guy embraced the lady -

'Lady, my dear, what has made you cry? Give me Beton, don't try to hide him!'

'My lord,' she said, 'let me explain! God in heaven be my witness, I can't give him to you. Some sailors came ashore and took him, then they sailed away with him. That's why you've found me looking so unhappy.'

'You'll soon change your tune!' said the murderer. He had a number of long thorns brought, and at once Ebrart had them sharpened to fine points and then driven into her breasts. A hundred sharp thorns they drove in, till blood and milk gushed out together. The noble girl cried out,

'Ah, my lord Guy, don't kill me! Daurel took him, that's all I can tell you.'

'That may be true,' said the traitor, 'for I didn't see him at dinner. Men, we'll go home now, it's late in the evening and we have nothing to eat. Tomorrow morning early we'll ride to Montclar. If the boy is in any place where I can find him, no one in the world shall keep him from me. We'll be at Aspremont by bedtime.'

Lady Aicelina - Jesus protect her! - was so badly beaten that there was no help to give her. Her brother arrived as the vespers bell was ringing and took her away, for he loved her dearly. Her father saw her as she came in, in such a condition that he wept.

'Lord Jesus Christ, I pray for Beton. Lord God, save him from death!'

26

Very early the traitor Guy got up. He picked a hundred of his best knights and ordered them to arms.

'At your command, my lord!' they answered. Fresh and well-rested, the warhorses were led out into the yard and the knights set foot in the gilded stirrups and mounted. Out in the lead rode Guy the renegade.

They reached Montclar after midday and halted below Daurel's ramparts, under the look-out posts, the pointed turrets and three crenellated towers. It was a place no one could ever take or storm. The gate was shut. Guy shouted, and inside the castle they heard him with alarm.

'Father,' said Daurel's sons, 'go out to him. Don't give him the child for anyone! We have enough silver and gold!'

'Well said, my good sons! I shall go out; you bar the gates. Whatever happens to me, do not promise him my dear lord. And if he kills me, this is what you must do: Wait until after dark and then at night get ropes and go down the rock to the sea. Take my lord away by boat and where God wants you to be, my dear sons, there he will bring you ashore.'

Daurel went out and they shut the gate. Guy said to him,

'Surely we can be friends! You have got Beton inside there; let me have him and I will give you one of my cities. I shall bring him up, and love him dearly.'

'My lord,' said Daurel, 'be sure of this: I shall not give him to you for any wealth you may offer, nor if you tear me limb from limb. He is my lord and I shall bring him up in peace.'

Then wicked Guy shouted,

'My knights, burn me the castle!' Ready to obey him, the knights fetched fire, but Daurel said,

'Wait! I'll go in, and bring him out to you soon.'

'A good decision!' said Guy.

Valiant Daurel went into the palace and faithless Guy remained outside, very angry. Daurel sat down on a bench, wept and tore his hair. He beat his breast and sides till blood spurted from his mouth.

'Wretch, unfortunate!' he cried. 'How stupid of me to come ashore here! If I give up the child, he'll be cut to pieces, and if I keep him, he'll burn!' His sons wept too, and collapsed unconscious. Daurel's wife went to him and said, weeping,

'My dear, how unhappy you are!'

'Yes, indeed, my lady, I ought never to have been born! I do not know what to do! My dearest, what do you suggest?'

'Sons,' said Beatrice, 'and all of you, listen! Do exactly what I am going to say.'

'Lady,' they answered, 'why not tell us straight out? We are ready, even before you speak. We'll do just as you command.'

'Look at this child lying here, your brother, my own son. He and Beton were born the same night. The duke who is dead baptised him. Now, wrap him in this silk coverlet, lift little Beton out of the cradle and take our son to the traitor. Let him do as he likes with him. My son will die, my lord will be saved.' All three responded,

'Praise be to God! Your plan is good, we approve it.'

Daurel went out, carrying his son in his arms. He was a handsome child, for he had been well fed on good milk.

'You must guarantee the boy's safety,' Daurel said to Guy. 'Promise you will never do him any harm.'

'You can be quite sure,' said the traitor, 'that I shan't hurt him, no, he shall be well looked after.' Daurel gave him the baby. Guy took it quickly and uncovered its face. 'Beton,' he said, 'you certainly escaped me. Soon you shall be well cared for.'

27

'Daurel,' said Guy, 'I shall never be your friend. You tried to hide my enemy from me.'

'I did what was right, my lord,' said Daurel. 'A vassal always owes love to his lord.'

'Look what I'll do with him,' said the traitor. He took the baby by its feet and swung it against a pillar, so that its eyes flew out and its brains were spattered about. 'There now, Beton,' said Guy, 'that will do! I'll never need to watch out for you any more.'

The bystanders could not bear it, they covered their faces and wept. Guy went away and left Montclar.

'What do you think?' they all said to each other. 'Lord Jesus Christ, how can you endure this?' And Daurel went to pick up his son and wrapped him in fine silk. I cannot tell you how he felt! He rode without stopping to Poitiers.

Lady Esmengart had just heard that Guy had killed her son and she was grieving bitterly. As she began to lament, Daurel came in carrying the baby and went to set it down in the courtyard. Everyone looked at it, and wept. Lady Esmengart was on the point of fainting; brave Daurel reassured her. He drew her aside and begged her to take heart.

'Lady,' he said, 'you have no need to be distressed, for it was I engendered him. By these eyes with which I see you, this was my son! I had the children exchanged. Mine is dead, yours is at nurse. Take charge of Montclar castle, for I shall go across the sea with your child and I don't think you'll see me here again until he's strong enough to bear arms.'

Three times the lady kissed him, and exclaimed,

'My fellow parent,* God guide and keep you! You have done what no one has ever done before, giving up your own son to save your lord!' The lady went to look at her godson. She knew him well and her grief broke out in lamentation.

* Esmengart was the dead baby's godmother and so she and Daurel were related as *commère* and *compère*, co-mother and co-father. The three kisses she gives him now are not just an effusion of gratitude, they echo the three kisses given as part of a marriage ceremony; see laisses 6 and 17.

No one ever saw a minstrel's son so nobly mourned! She had the boy buried next to the duke. He had died for him, and well deserved that honour.

Now brave Daurel returned to Montclar where he quickly had a ship prepared, stocking it with food and drink and an ample supply of weapons. His harp and viol too, he took with him for pleasure, as well as a wet-nurse for the child, his palfrey and his dappled horse, nor did he leave his squire behind. His two sons wept. The sails were set, the ship put out to sea. Daurel's wife climbed up the tower and watched till they were out of sight. Then she became very distressed -

'Alas, wretch that I am, now what am I do? My son is dead, I shall never get him back, I can see my little lord sailing away, and my husband too, who ought to take charge of me!' She threw herself down, never to stand up again. Her sons ran to help her, but she died. The Lord God be kind to her!

Now let us leave Daurel and little Beton and talk about the seneschal Sir Azemar.

28

Lady Esmengart sent for her servant, Sir Azemar, who came running, his eyes wet with tears.

'Lady,' he said, 'I am so unhappy about Beton's death! That unbelieving traitor has killed him.'

'Don't distress yourself, friend,' she said. 'Please God, Beton is certainly alive. We can be happy, for Daurel has taken him away by sea. He put his own little son in Beton's place. You are to take charge of Montclar, where Daurel's sons must stand at bay. Here is plenty of gold for you, plenty of silver: fortify the tower, command the garrison. Provide good supplies of oats, rye and wheat, of meat, wine, wafers and spiced honey-wine. Lay in stocks for fifteen years, for within a dozen years there will be more than a hundred of you there. Have sufficient arms and other equipment. Be there yourself, friend, day and night. If any attack you, acquit yourselves well. No living soul will capture you! I am certain that before twelve years have passed Beton and Daurel will return, will come back with horsemen and footsoldiers, will kill the unbelieving traitor, and make a great and wealthy man of you.'

'Lady,' he said, 'I shall always obey your orders without fail, I am eager and happy to serve you. I will command the castle well and carefully. How relieved and glad I am to know that little Beton is alive!'

29

And Sir Azemar, valiant and light of foot, filled all the granaries with clean wheat and laid in load after load of oats and hay for the swift warhorses. Four thousand sides of good salt pork he had brought in, and as much good wine as they would need. He installed thirty archers, twenty crossbowmen and forty picked knights and maintained all of them and their wives nobly. Goshawks and sparrowhawks were kept there, as well as hounds for hunting and fast coursers. They played gambling games of backgammon and chess. There in the castle they led a merry life. Now the lying traitor has a war on his hands!

30

When wicked Guy heard that brave Daurel had got Beton away and that Montclar was garrisoned, he tugged at his beard and tore his furred robe. He knew now that he would have to fight. He went to Lady Esmengart and spoke to her; he imprisoned her in a tower and kept her there a year in great discomfort. He summoned his host, a thousand knights and more, and rode fast to Montclar, then examined the towers and rode all round. The defenders did not count him worth a button. Brave and gallant were Daurel's sons, and they defended themselves like men. Together they shouted out aloud:

'We think nothing of him, that foul traitor Guy who killed the duke and tried to kill Beton!'

Then Sir Azemar cried,

'Guy, traitor, murderer, you can't ever be forgiven. Why don't you get away to some other land? My lord is alive! You have no hope, you skulking thief who killed your own lord!'

'By God, fellow,' said Guy, 'you'll be sorry you said that! By the Lord who made the sky and the firmament, I'll hang you all from a single beam!'

Bertrand, Daurel's son, called back,

'That's a lie at any rate! We can defend ourselves against a traitor like you!'

'Antona!' they shouted with the utmost joy. And when Guy saw there was nothing he could do, he went away raging.

Let us leave Montclar and Guy the traitor; we will speak of Daurel and the child Beton.

31

Away went Daurel, full of joy, strong and vigorous, over the deep sea. But he had no idea that his noble wife had thrown herself from the top of the high tower and died in the lofty palace. Great will be his sorrow when he finds out!

The baby began to cry, distressing Daurel, so he picked up his viol and played a love song.

'Ah,' he said, 'my little gentle lord,
how far you are travelling from your great honour! *
In what great dishonour are we fleeing from it!
For you I have given my youngest son,
you I have snatched from the traitor's hands.
Duke's son, emperor's nephew,
and look at us, running away like robbers!
You have no brother, no sister,
who can ever avenge this dishonour.'

Saying this, he could not help weeping, and in love and joy he kissed the child. 'Lord Jesus Christ, in your kindness bring us to a good safe haven and keep us from harm and sorrow!'

* 'Honour' in the sense of 'fief'. Daurel is playing on the words 'honour' and 'dishonour'.

32

In Babylon*, God be praised for it, Daurel came ashore in a fine harbour. He went to the emir's palace, with his squire carrying the child in his arms. The emir had just risen from table; five hundred renowned knights were present. Daurel entered and gave courteous greeting:

'God save the king who is emir and duke, God save the queen and these knights!'

'Minstrel, come in!' they answered. 'Happy be the hour that brings you!'

Daurel came forward and performed several numbers, some of one kind, some of another, for he knew a very great many. Next he took his harp and played two lays, then entertained them on the viol, and gave a display of leaping and tumbling. They were all delighted and the king himself was very pleased.

'My lord,' said Daurel, 'listen to me! I have come here all the way from France to serve you, because the nobles of King Charles' court give you such high praise. You are the best king ever known! Kings and counts, I have quitted them all and come ashore here for your sake. I shall stay with you as long as you live.'

* 'Babylon' was the name given in medieval times to Cairo. Daurel is coming ashore in Alexandria.

The king, who was sitting down, stood up.

'Friend,' he said, 'tell me your name.'

'May it please you, my lord, my name is Daurel.'

'Daurel,' said the king, 'stay with me, and I will give you one of my cities. You shall have silver and gold enough and to spare.'

'My lord,' said Daurel, 'you are very generous, but I do not want wealth. All I ask is that you should have this child brought up for me. He is my son, my darling. My wife, to my great sorrow, is dead.' He thought he was lying, but this was true.

'Show him to me,' said the king. Daurel handed him the child, and he took him readily and lifted the silk wrap. At this, the baby opened his eyes and laughed. The king was delighted.

'Child,' he said, 'what a happy nature you have! You have never seen me before, and how cheerful you are! You shall be most honourably cared for. My queen,' he said to his wife, 'take charge of him. As you love me, cherish him.'

'Give him here into my arms, my lord,' she said. 'By that Lord who formed us all, he shall be as well suckled and cared for as if I had carried him in my own womb.'

The lady took him and he was kept safe and secret. Until he was three, he lived in the queen's rooms, carefully guarded. Then he went out and was much admired.

Everyone looked at him, for he was remarkably beautiful - well proportioned, with fair hair, eyes grey as a moulted falcon, throat fresh as a summer rose, white like snow, and he had a noble face.

'Listen, my knights,' said the king. 'This boy cannot be Daurel's son! There's no resemblance, none at all.' Joining them, Daurel said,

'My lord king, you don't think much of me, calling my son a bastard!'

'No, Daurel, don't be angry,' said the king. 'So help me charity, I meant no harm!'

When Beton was four, everyone thought the world of him. He went and sat down by the king, caught hold of his gloves and took them away from him. (They were of cloth trimmed all round with gold). Beton took them from the king and without a moment's hesitation went and offered them to the queen. She accepted them and kissed the child's eyes. The king laughed and said,

'Listen to me - I'd give thirteen of my cities to have a son like this boy, surely a future emir! He'd make a much better emir's child than the son of a minstrel of poor heredity.'

When he was five, Beton was well grown, well educated and valiant. He could ride horses and gallop them; he could talk well and converse intelligently, he played chess, backgammon and dice, and everyone in the emir's court loved him dearly.

Let us leave Beton and Daurel in peace and return to those we were speaking of earlier.

33

The traitor Guy was riding along the riverbank, with over a hundred men to guard him. They took good care to bring their weapons with them, as well as ten falcons to fly at cranes. A spy went and reported this to the men of Montclar and they ran to arms, put on hauberks and bright helmets and took good swords with which to strike great blows. In the lead rode Sir Azemar, with Bertrand, the minstrel's son, beside him. They rode out and arrayed themselves for battle, leaving ten men to defend the castle.

'My lords,' said Sir Azemar, 'this is what I want you to do: let us go and look for them in Dark Valley. That's where we'll find them, flying their falcons.'

Guy looked up and saw the riders coming. He left the falcons and hurried to put on his armour, shouting to his followers,

'Look out, men! Here are those wretches from Montclar!' At these words they went to arm. Up rode Bertrand on a dapple grey, spurring with all his might and shouting,

'Guy, false traitor, you can't escape me! You killed my brother, the baby you dashed against a pillar! I require his death of you!' The count heard him, mounted his horse and charged. Great blows they struck and both shields flew to pieces. Bertrand's blow almost brought Guy down, but it was Bertrand who fell.

'There,' said Guy, 'filthy juggler's son! Don't ever challenge a count again!' Bertrand's comrades raced to his help, yelling aloud as they lowered their lances. What an encounter you would have seen then, spears splintering, shields shattered, tunics ripped and linked mail torn! Up rode courteous Sir Azemar, lowered his pennon, charged and struck Guy, but could not unseat him.

'Antona!' he shouted. 'Soon you'll see Beton, the child you thought you'd killed!'

The count heard this. Frantic with rage, he drew his sword, rode full tilt and struck a young man on his shining helmet. Down through his teeth he drove the blade and flung him dead, never to move again. He charged the men of Montclar and scattered them.

'To me, Aspremont!' he shouted. 'No one I've struck ever comes back for more!'

34

Bertrand heard this and it made him angry. He spurred his horse, it danced and sprang forward, but Sir Azemar was near despair. Shields held firm and sharp spearpoints lowered, fifteen of them charged Count Guy. Three struck home on his close-woven mailshirt; his shield saved him from the others. They all landed their blows, but Count Guy sat firm and did not even lose a stirrup. He struck one of them and threw him down dead. Bertrand saw the man fall; raging, he spurred his warhorse, drew his glittering sword and struck hard at Guy's bright pointed helmet, sending its two side-pieces tumbling down. Attackers or attacked, none would draw back, all fought fiercely.

35

Up rode agile Sir Azemar, leading a charge of four knights; three struck home on Count Guy's quartered shield and moistened their pennons in his blood. But Sir Azemar struck Guy's horse; it fell and the count fell with it to the ground, but kept his senses. From all sides they rained fierce blows on him, but Guy caught and parried them on his sharp steel. Any man he struck fell to the ground. They very much feared his powerful blows: they watched but did not dare touch him. Then Bertrand shouted,

'Come on, men, this lying traitor, surely we can get him down!' Eagerly they all attacked him and soon had his shield in pieces. As Bertrand was speaking, a knight of Guy's called Geoffrey charged Requier and used his strong spear to thrust him off his horse. Then he grasped the charger's reins and forced his way through the mêlée shouting,

'Mount, Count Guy, you must remount!'

Guy vaulted up, eager to continue, but his men could not hold; they turned and fled along the high road. The men of Montclar pursued them, striking their heads off, slashing and bringing them down. Seven they killed and twenty they took prisoner. And false Guy, once he got clear, did not draw rein till he reached Aspremont. The men of Montclar went home with their prisoners, and made them swear on holy relics that they would help them in the war and would never be false or untrue.

36

Wretched and furious was Count Guy, the traitor. He summoned the vassals from his fiefs and mustered them - one thousand and three hundred knights, there were, and over a thousand picked sergeants. He rode without halt to Montclar and there set his unjust siege. Tents were pitched all round the castle, trebuchets and mangonels built. But nothing they did could harm the defenders. Then Guy's men swore on holy relics: not for any living man would they go away until they had captured the men in Montclar.

The defenders inside the place yelled and shouted,

'Ah Guy, you traitor, wicked and faithless, you'll soon break your false oaths!'

Inside the castle all was cheerfulness and joy, day and night they rejoiced and were glad. They had enough food to last for twelve years, and water to turn mills, gushing and running clear. Twelve years they would all stay there safely enclosed until Beton took arms.

Let us leave Montclar and the siege.

At six years old Beton was a handsome and noble child, fresh-complexioned, with bright laughing eyes. The king loved him dearly, and so did the queen and their daughter. The girl had charming manners and was very pretty; her name was Erimena.

Now brave Daurel was thoroughly contented. He called the boy and said to him kindly,

'Beton, dear son, learn to play the harp and the viol, they will give you great pleasure.'

'My lord, dear father,' answered Beton like a well brought up child, 'as you command. Here I am, ready to do as you wish.'

37

At seven years old Beton could play the viol well, also the citole, and was a fine harpist. He could sing songs and compose them himself too.

One day Daurel happened to go out in a boat after dolphins. Young Beton saw some children playing, sons of rich men, and he raced off at once and pawned his tunic, then went running to the games table and sat down. The courtiers went to tell the king, who began to watch. Before Beton rose, God gave him such success that he stripped ten boys of their tunics, absolutely refusing to let them keep them. He slung them over his shoulder and went off. The king called one of his young men to him.

'Friend,' he said, 'go and see what he does with those tunics he's carrying.'

'My lord,' said the young man, 'I shall certainly find out.'

Beton went out and began to shout all over the town,

'Anyone who wants a tunic, come and ask me!' He gave them all away to noble youngsters and went back into the palace, where he said jokingly,

'You're going to shiver, boys! Believe me, you'd better go and get some more made.'*

The young man reported all this, just as he had seen it, to the emir, who then summoned his whole court: let all who loved him be present. More than a hundred thousand people gathered, including the queen, a most estimable lady.

'Barons,' said the king, 'what is your opinion of that child standing over there, young Beton, whom I love so dearly? Such signs of early prowess I see in him! He wins ten tunics at play and the moment he's got them, he goes and gives them away. By that Lord who gave us all the gift of speech, I will not believe that he's a minstrel's son! I have seen him riding horses at full gallop, I've seen him putting on mailshirts and taking them off; shields too, he'll hold them and set them on his arm.'

'I'll test it for you,' said the queen. 'Send him into the private quarters to recite poems to my daughter. I'll have a hundred marks of silver offered him, and if he takes it, he's a minstrel's son, and if not, he's nothing of the kind.'

All agreed to this plan, and the king sent for the boy. Beton came at once and knelt down.

* This follows Meyer's interpretation. Kimmel and Lee take the verbs *tremolar* and *talhar* as gaming terms, and conclude that an unidentified speaker is saying, 'You'll really know how to shake [the dice, when you are older], believe me, you'll fleece many others'.

'Beton,' said the emir, 'I'd like you to go and amuse my daughter. Take your viol and play some of your lays. She is feeling sad, go and cheer her up for me.'

'My lord,' said the boy, 'I shall be glad to do so.' He ran off, took his viol and began to tune it. The queen went to tell her daughter what to do.

'Child,' she said, 'I want a word with you. I'm going to leave a hundred marks of silver here with you, because young Beton is coming to entertain you. Give him the silver when he goes away.'

The king spoke to his courtiers:

'Barons, let's go and listen, we'll see how he manages this.' They concealed themselves all round the private quarters, so as to hear what would happen.

38

Up into the private quarters went Beton, wearing a fine tunic, handsomely laced. Erimena jumped up and exclaimed,

'Come in, friend, and welcome!' Young and very beautiful, not yet ten years old, she was in a happy mood, tossing three golden dice in her hand.

'Lady,' said Beton, 'my lord the emir has sent me to you, and I am very glad he has. I know some fine poems, and I'd like you to hear some of them.' He recited his verses and was heard attentively. The king listened from his hiding place and so, close beside him, did the queen. So too did a hundred good knights; they all listened to see how Beton behaved. He stayed there some time, entertaining Erimena; he sang and played the viol and enjoyed himself very much.

'Lady,' he said, 'I'll go now, if you please. Always send for me, my lady, whenever you want me.'

'Listen a moment, Beton,' she said, and put the hundred marks of silver down in front of him. 'Friend, please take this. You can use it to buy a stable-kept palfrey. It's my first gift, you won't refuse it!'

'Lady,' he said, 'a thousand thanks and a hundred blessings! How can I need silver and gold? It's enough to know that you care about me! Minstrels will come from many lands, from near and far - give this wealth to them, my lady, and they'll sing your praises in distant kingdoms and make you famous there. You have overpaid me already, for you are always generous to me, and my lord the emir brought me up.'

'Beton,' she said, 'by the faith you bear me, you shall not go away without something of mine!'

'Oh lady,' he said, 'why do you insist? Anything I took would only embarrass me. But to please you - and for no other reason! - I'll take these dice from your hand.'

'You ask for very little, friend!' she said. 'Take them, then, and keep them for kindness' sake.' She held them out and he took them.

'Give me leave, lady,' he said, and she answered,

'Go with good luck, Beton, and God give you your heart's desire!'

'Lady,' he replied, 'God be with you here!'

Beton went out and happened to meet the boys who were taking the stabled warhorses to be watered. Seeing them, he ran straight to the stable, took out the king's own horse, mounted it and went with the others to water it.

The king left the hiding place where he had been listening to Beton, and then he saw him riding his horse.

'Look there, my lords,' he said. 'I'm sure it's impossible for that boy to be Daurel's son!'

'No, indeed,' they all answered. 'By the Lord who made us all, he's the son of a duke, a king or an emir.'

'Barons,' he said, 'why don't you call him here?' They called him, and he came at once.

'Beton,' said the king, 'how could you dare even to touch my warhorse?'

'My lord,' said Beton, 'he has had nothing to drink all day and your squire is very clumsy. With your permission, I'll take him to the water.'

'Beton,' said the king, 'I put you in charge of my horse.'

'My lord,' answered Beton, 'I'll take good care of him.' He

went away, and all present exclaimed together,

'This child was stolen, we are sure of it!'

That day Beton was tested, and from then on they loved him a thousand times more dearly than before.

39

When Beton was nine years old he was the king's squire, handsome, well made and well spoken. He played backgammon and chess for money, went hunting with hounds and greyhounds, with goshawks and sparrowhawks, rode with lowered lance and galloped the warhorses. The king loved him, the queen adored him and their charming daughter was devoted to him. Great ladies, young noblemen and knights, everyone loved him. He served at table, stood ready before the king and instantly brought him anything he needed, and afterwards was happy to play the viol and sing for them. Daurel watched all this and was delighted.

40

At eleven years old Beton was a fine swordsman and used to practise with the knights of that neighbourhood. Good Daurel took great care of him: he bought him a horse and also arms and armour, very handsome, small and light-weight.

Then Daurel sent for a Saracen who was experienced in training boys and said to him,

'Friend, listen to me.' He sent for young Beton as well, and then said to the Saracen, 'Teach this son of mine to fight. I know you want to help him improve.' The Saracen took Beton with him and taught him how to use his sword, how to vault onto his warhorse from the ground, how to use his shield both to protect himself and to attack, how to plant heavy blows on the other man's shield, how to shatter and to brandish straight spear-shafts, how to control and manage warhorses, to give and parry strong blows, and how to behave in the press of battle. All one year he taught him, till there was nothing left to teach and Beton knew how to fight and use weapons.

41

Beton at twelve years old had excellent judgement, as Daurel was delighted to observe. He called the boy, and Beton came at once.

'Dear son,' he said, 'be quick now, get your weapons, your good armour and the fast warhorses. You and I are going to ride out together.'

'Father, dear sir, at your command! All shall be done as you wish.'

The two of them rode together into a fine green meadow.

'Now my good son,' said Daurel, 'take care, put your armour on.' Beton did so well and carefully. All duly armed, he asked Daurel, laughing,

'My lord, father, what are you planning?'

'Dear son,' he said, 'I am going to test your courage. In God's name now, seriously, you will joust with me.'

'My dear lord, you are talking nonsense! How could I ever raise my shining spear against you? Not for a hundred thousand marks of silver could I do such a thing!'

'Do it you shall, though, by almighty God! Don't be afraid of hitting me, for I shall use my full strength against you.'

Each of them withdrew a measured furlong, lowered his spear and struck with great force. Both drove their spearheads through the shields and into the mailshirts, which saved them from death. Daurel thrust powerfully, and so did the boy, forcing Daurel to the ground. Beton rode on and made his turn very neatly, and Daurel under his shining helmet laughed in delight.

'Good luck to such youth, Beton!' he said. 'Now I'm sure that all is well. Ah, Lord God, how I thank you for this!' The boy dismounted, weeping with all his heart, and he came up to Daurel and caught hold of his hand.

'Ah, father, dear sir, how foolish of you to confront me! If I had killed you, I would kill myself too!'

'My dear son,' said Daurel, 'now you know for certain that you will be a true fighter, if you live long.' Together they laid their armour aside and went and sat down on the green grass.

42

'Dear Beton,' said Daurel the minstrel, 'whose son are you? Can you tell me?'

'Sir, yours, and so I wish to be!'

'No, my dear, not so, by God who gave me speech. No, you are my lord, but you must keep it secret. You are well grown and handsome, fit to bear arms. You are duke and count. I'll explain - you are nephew to great Charles, the best king ever known, his sister's son. You owe Charles no love, none at all, for it was he who drove you into landless exile. Your father the duke gave me Montclar, a strong castle standing by the sea. A traitor, a count called Guy, killed your father when they were out hunting together, then he bought your mother for a huge sum of silver and gold. You were cared for on an island in the sea. Guy the traitor had you hunted for and found; he meant to kill you, but I stole you away. We had no chance of escape, until I gave up my own little son instead of you. Before my very eyes Guy dashed him against a pillar so that his eyes flew out of their sockets. Guy thought it was you he had murdered. After seeing that, I could bear no more; I fled, because I hoped I could save you.'

Young Beton broke out crying.

'Sir', he exclaimed, 'how could you do that? How can I ever repay you?'

'My dear lord, I can tell you how! Very soon now we shall go home, we shall kill Guy, he cannot escape us. The whole of Poitiers will come in to you, Bordeaux, Antona, all the country as far as Montclar. I left two sons in Montclar castle for your sake, and my wife is there too. Do as I shall tell you, not as you feel inclined, and you won't go wrong. Keep your identity completely secret until you are ready to leave.'

'Dear father, all shall be as you command.'

Picking up their weapons, they returned to the palace, where they played their viols for the king and made merry. Young Beton knelt and laid his instrument down before the king.

43

When Beton was thirteen he was strong and well respected, much in demand at court and honoured by the best people.

Now King Gormon summoned his barons. There was great enmity between this king and the emir; twenty years they had been at war. Gormon mounted a massive attack, bringing with him more than twelve thousand good knights and a hundred thousand men, for none of them wanted to stay behind. He came ashore in Babylon and the town was in uproar. Young Beton knew what to do: he ran to fetch the king's warhorse, saddled and bridled him and led him to the king.

'My lord,' he said, 'why don't you mount? Your horse is properly saddled.'

'Take him back, Beton,' said the king. 'We shall not go out, we are not armed, we are few and they are many. It would be the height of folly to go out.'

'My lord,' he said, 'as you command!' and he turned away, angry. He remembered his ancestry, flung on the king's own mailshirt, girded on his sword, crossed himself three times, laced on the gold-rimmed helmet and from the ground where he stood, leapt onto the horse. Well equipped with the royal arms and armour, he took the shield, thick-studded and adorned with four gold tines, and brandished the spear, with its head of nielloed steel.

Beton wears the king's armour, drives gilt spurs into the king's charger and makes straight for the gateway.

'Open the gates!' he tells the gatekeeper. 'Let the king and all his barons see!' The man obeys him and cries,

'God be with you!'

The king had gone up to the windows. He saw the boy riding at full gallop, realised who it was and stood astonished.

'My queen, look out there! Look at Beton! He's wearing my armour, riding my charger - is he out of his mind?'

'Please God, no, my lord!' she said. 'By the faith you owe me, commend him to God! If he lives, I tell you, he'll be a wonderful support to us! If he's taken, we'll pay any ransom!'

Now from the main host came two picked knights, riding towards the ditches. Beton saw and wheeled to meet them. All along the ramparts and ditches, his friends watched. Beton shouted,

'Sirs, don't run away! One of you draw aside, I'll joust with him, whichever you like. You'll lose your warhorse or win this one.'

'Comrade,' cried one of them, 'joust with me!' Spearpoints lowered, both spurred and struck great blows on the good strong-rimmed shields. The infidel struck him well, driving his point into the hauberk. Beton hit him like an experienced knight, knocked down his shield and ripped his mailshirt. In the sight of all the watchers, the heathen fell.

'You're quite right to tumble!' cried Beton. 'It was a minstrel who struck you!' *

The man's comrade saw him fall and was angry and ashamed. He spurred and rode full tilt at Beton, who unflinchingly brandished the spear with its inlaid steel. Such strong and pitiless blows they both delivered that their shields flew into fragments. The infidel hit hard, but so did the boy, and he sent the gilt saddlebows flying and tossed the heathen down onto the meadow.

'Friend,' he said, 'tell Sir Gormon from me that a minstrel's son sent you both tumbling!'

The king and all his nobles were watching.

'Listen, my knights!' he cried. 'By that Lord who made us all, if he lives another year, he'll be an emir!'

All this was seen from Gormon's host, and more than three thousand men rode forward, but Beton did not wait for them. He rode back, calm and collected, leading the two saddled chargers. The report spread fast all over the town and in the private quarters. Beton behaved very properly and gave the warhorses away to two young men. He disarmed in the

* A rare example of battlefield humour, the despised minstrels being also acrobats or tumblers.

courtyard and everyone gazed at him because he was so handsome.

Daurel came running up grasping a thick, squared stick.

'You wretched minstrel's son,' he cried, 'by the Lord who made us all, you did wrong to go out without my orders!' The boy gave him a well-bred answer:

'Father, my lord, why are you angry? It gives me such joy, why do you blame me?' Everyone cried out,

'Daurel, don't be angry! Look how well the boy answers you!' Soon there was a crowd round them, and the king came with all his nobles.

44

The king rode up as fast as his palfrey could carry him, came up to Daurel and took hold of his head.

'By that Lord who made us all, into my prison you shall go and stay there a dozen years - it's dark, you'll see nothing, for two months you'll eat nothing, no bread, no wine, no food at all - if you don't tell me whose son this is! He's not yours, so God and the faith help me!' Brave and courteous, Daurel answered,

'Ah, my lord king, for God's sake be merciful! Summon your court at once, the knights and the leading citizens, and then I'll declare whose son he is. Not mine, you are quite right. There's no duke, count or king of nobler descent in all the world!' And so the emir ordered an infidel to blow for a proclamation - let all come promptly to the high palace.

45

To court they came, saints, sinners and all. Brave Daurel stepped up onto a rostrum and began to speak:

'My lords! My lord king and you, all his barons, listen to me! None of you speak a word! You see this boy in the furred tunic - I tell you truly, he is count and duke. He is the son of Bevis duke of Antona, to whom God grant grace! He is also nephew to the emperor Charles, greatest king that is or ever has been. Charles gave his sister to Bevis, and to Duke Bevis was born the child Beton. His father the duke took as comrade a count of his called Guy, who most treacherously killed him and then by force, against her will, took the fair and noble Lady Esmengart, the child's mother. Beton was kept hidden on an island out at sea. Villainous Guy sought to kill him, and in time discovered his hiding place. I removed the baby and took him to my own house. Wickedly that traitor followed me and demanded the child from me. I told him, 'No'. He tried to burn both myself and the child. And I, when I could see no other remedy, instead of Beton gave him one of my own sons. In the sight of all present, he took him by the heels, struck him against the wall and dashed his brains out. I am Beton's vassal, I made him that gift. Then I fled away here into your land. You have brought him up and I am grateful.

We shall go away now, it is full time, and take vengeance on the foul traitor Guy. No one who injures Beton will find forgiveness, for his prowess is already clear.'

46

When the king heard all this and realised that he had been bringing up the nephew of Charlemagne all these years, he went to Beton, took him in his arms and kissed him a hundred times, and so too did the queen. All his nobles cried out,

'King, give him your daughter, it's a most suitable match!' The king was delighted, and said, laughing,

'Beton, I offer you my daughter.' Very courteously the boy replied,

'My lord, indeed I don't refuse her! With the approval of my father who gave me arms, I shall be delighted to accept her.' Emphatically Daurel exclaimed,

'Accept her, my lord, it's an admirable match! Make just one condition: that for love of you she'll agree to be baptised. You shall certainly take her to Poitiers.'

The queen went running into the private rooms, caught hold of her lovely daughter and in the sight of them all drew her into the meeting. Then before five hundred witnesses she asked,

'Lady Erimena, do you wish to be baptised? Beton wants you to, so that he can marry you.' Courteously Lady Erimena answered,

'Yes, my lady, I do, if that's what Beton wants.'

'King,' said Daurel, 'give him some of your forces, three thousand or more fighting men, each one fully equipped, and we'll leave for Poitiers in a fortnight's time, and avoid delay. Beton will take vengeance on his enemies, and afterwards he will receive the lady; you shall give her to him with great celebrations.' Everyone cried out that this was very fitting, and then together they all shouted,

'King, have it sworn now, in our presence!'

'Beton,' said the king, 'take the oath!'

'My lord,' he said, 'I shan't argue! Let my father Daurel take it first.' The king himself accepted their good faith. The two of them swore on a sword and Daurel on a silver cross.

Then and there without delay they prepared the ships, filling them with excellent weapons and everything needed on board. Ten thousand and three hundred men, they were, if not more. Beton took leave and with his strong force put out to sea. They hoisted their sails, God gave them a fair wind, and for three full months they sailed without storms across the sea. Then, joyful and happy, they made landfall near Montclar.

47

Now Daurel looked and saw Montclar. They came to land there, meaning to enter the castle, but all around them they saw the siege set, the tents pitched and cooking fires smoking. Seeing this, Daurel pointed and said,

'My lord, God's doing us great honour! It doesn't look as if we need go to much trouble, we can take vengeance on our enemies here and now. Look, Guy's there, he can't escape us. If you'll take my advice, you will order your men to arm.'

'My lord,' said Beton, 'as you command.' Every man went to arms, none needed to be told twice.

Now those in the castle were looking out and valiant Daurel showed them his shield. They knew it well and you would have seen them rejoicing and telling each other,

'It's my lord, he's come from across the sea!' They armed themselves for a sortie.

'Let's be ready when we hear them shout!'

And Beton armed himself; he put on a good light mailshirt and took his sword; he would certainly not forget that. In eager haste, Daurel took another. Daurel had grown his beard long, longer than one could imagine; for seven years he had not had it cut.

Quickly brave Daurel arrayed the men, then with courtesy gave them their orders:

'No one is to spur forward! Stand until you hear us shout, and then ride, don't wait for anyone else!'

Daurel wrapped himself in a great cloak and made young Beton do the same. They carried viols, like minstrels. Good Daurel advised Beton:

'My lord, so that you know what to do: I shall sing and you must listen. I shall use words that will make him angry, and I think he'll attack me.'

'And I'll take vengeance!' said Beton.

Without hesitation they went straight to the tent. As they entered, Guy was at table.

'Minstrels,' he called, 'come and eat!'

'We hope to entertain you,' said Daurel. Young Beton began to play a pleasant tune and brave Daurel sang:

'Who'll hear a song, I'll tell him, I believe,
of a betrayal that must not be hid,
of wicked Guy, forsworn and treacherous -
may Jesus spurn him! -
who killed the duke when they went out to hunt.'

Guy had a knife in his hand; he went to throw it at Daurel, but Beton tossed viol and cloak aside, drew his sword and with one blow sent Guy's right arm flying to the ground.

'Antona!' Beton cried aloud and clear. 'You are all my vassals, let none dare oppose us!'

Inside the castle they heard him, opened the gates and came out to join him. The forces from beyond the sea spurred forward, and there was nothing left to do but harass the enemy. What heads you would have seen slashed off, what men topple and fall, knights overthrown and dying, fists and feet flying across the field! But Daurel went to protect the men on foot:

'No one dare touch them! The traitor Guy forced them to serve him.' He allowed all the horsemen to be killed; happy were any who got away, not one waiting for a friend.

Young Beton had Guy firmly bound and a rope flung round his neck. Daurel's sons came to kiss their father and then embraced their lord. What rejoicing you would have seen there!

Then good Daurel asked,

'Where is my wife, my darling?'

'Not here, not here!' they answered. 'She died as soon as she had seen you go.'

Hearing that, Daurel could not keep on his feet; he fell unconscious and they ran to comfort him. Young Beton saw

Daurel's anguish and wept for grief. They all tried to console Daurel and reproached him for his outcry.

'You have your sons,' they said, 'you must be happy with them!'

... to go to Poitiers.*

Brave Daurel had Guy tied to the tail of a strong dappled horse. Reaching Poitiers, they had horns blown and proclamations made. The townspeople set the church bells ringing and all came out in their best clothes to welcome Beton. The citizens praised God because he had given them back their lord. What great joy you would have seen displayed, what fine carpets thrown down in the streets! Whichever way you looked, there was joy and jubilation.

'Ah Lord God, we owe you great praise for bringing our lord back to us!'

Lady Esmengart heard the noise, looked out from the high palace and saw Guy all bloody at the horse's tail. Out she ran to discover what was happening. She found a youngster who could tell her:

'Good news for you, my lady! Look, here's your son come

* From now on the ms is increasingly illegible owing to water stains and wormholes. The next three lines contain scattered phrases indicating that Beton and his friends now ride for Poitiers. Words in italics translate probable readings of the damaged ms. Dots indicate omissions.

home from across the sea and he's had Guy the traitor dragged at his horse's heels.'

The lady heard this and did not wait a moment. She found her son and hurried to kiss him, as valiant Daurel named him to her. Then at once they delivered wicked Guy into her charge.

'Lady,' said Daurel, 'have this traitor guarded!'

'Up with him into the wind!' said the lady.

'I'll make him admit,' said Daurel, 'that he killed the good duke. He shall be avenged!'

Young Beton sent his troops to quarters. Joyfully they went up to the palace and stayed there all night until ... Valiant Beton assembled his court. He had the wicked fisherman .... that is, Ebrart, who ....

48

The people of Poitiers had their own lord restored to them, and the whole city rejoiced together. Very early in the morning they went to him and took many fine gifts - one gave him a palfrey, another a stable-kept horse, others gold cups or rich ring-embroidered silks. In great joy they assembled, and gave back to him all the fortified places of the realm and all the towns of the duchy. He is count and duke and this they have acknowledged.

In came the citizen who had yearned to see him, because the duke his father had always honoured him. He brought Lady Aicelina and her excellent young brother. Lady Aicelina spoke to Beton,

'My dear son,' she said, 'how I have longed for you! I have given you a hundred kisses, you can be sure! So wrongly, so wickedly they tortured me! That traitor and renegade I see there in chains, how sorely he beat me! Now I see you safe and sound, but I have not forgotten what they did to me! Give me Ebrart, the spy who found you.'

'Lady,' he said, 'you shall certainly have him.' Then he took her in his arms and kissed her like an old friend. He knew her well from all that Daurel had told him. Before she left he made *her a generous gift*: a fine castle, *rich and strong*.

The wicked fisherman *they skinned alive*.

From all sides *they crowded round* and young Beton *addressed Guy*:

'Speak, miserable count, let's hear the truth! Admit that you killed the duke.'

'My lord,' he said, 'I won't hide it. Yes, like a fool I killed him.' Good Daurel spoke urgently to Beton:

'Noble count, don't be sorry for him! Give him to me, let me avenge my son. Guy murdered him; I'll repay that!'

'Yes, as you wish,' answered Beton. In the sight of them all Daurel tied Guy to the tail of a fresh warhorse, dragged him to and fro all across Poitiers and finally flung him into a ditch. Little good did Guy get by it, for ravens and vultures ate what was left of him.

49

All are delighted to have recovered their own true lord. Young Beton spoke to Daurel:

'My lord, dear father, ... I put you in charge of all my lands. *Any man who is not your friend*, neither is he mine; any who love you, I will love.' To his loyal supporter Sir Azemar, he gave Aspremont, an important stronghold. Bertrand he made a knight, giving him full control of two castles, and the younger brother he made a squire.

......

Then Beton sent for his noble wife and with her came more than a thousand knights. He let her keep her name, as he did not want to change it, and she is known as the Lady Erimena.*

* A convert would usually receive a specifically Christian name at baptism, as Queen Bramimonde in the *Song of Roland* took the name Juliana. The emir's daughter keeps her own name, with its anagrammatic hint of her father's status.

The count married her at St Hilary's church and they lived always in great joy together.

50

It was the month of May, when trees break into flower and bushes smell sweet again. Count Beton flourished, strong and valiant. He went to visit his mother, kissed her lovingly and said,

'Lady, I shall be very unhappy if I can't take vengeance on the wicked emperor who supported Guy, that traitor who murdered my father and caused such unhappiness. He sold you most shamefully to that foul traitor, who *married you* and killed Daurel's *little son.* If I had not fled to that friendly king who gave me his fair daughter, he would have killed me, I would have been at his mercy. On Guy I'm avenged, thank God! But I'm no son of Bevis the warrior if I don't lay waste the emperor's lands before the month is out! And he is my uncle, may God disgrace him!'

'May God give you courage, son!' said the lady. 'The emperor is so powerful. His greatest vassals are your kinsmen. There ought not to be *ill feeling* between the two of you. Send a messenger on your fastest warhorse, tell Charles to do you right in respect of the great dishonour he did when he gave *his sister to Guy.* ..Within ten years let him raise his oriflamme. You have right and lordship against them; a hundred thousand knights will ride with you. The emir will bring you strong support.'

'God do you honour,' said the count, 'for no man ever had a better mother! I mean to avenge the great duke, your lord, and I shall do it, lady, without waste of time.'

51

Count Beton gave orders to Bertrand.

'Friend,' he said, 'go and put on your armour. Take two brave knights with you, Sir Azemar and Gauseran. Ride fast to the emperor. Don't greet him, don't offer any courtesy, simply say that I defy him, that I am not asking him for any agreement or truce, because he allowed me to be disinherited. Fifteen pack beasts loaded with gold and silver he took for my mother, he sold her for that. By God's mercy, I am ... I consider him neither my lord nor my kinsman. As long as I can bear arms, while I live he shall have no peace. Greet Roland the paladin from me, and for friendship's sake give him a glove of mine. He is my kinsman and should do me no harm.'

...

...

...

'As you command,' said Sir Azemar. 'We will uphold your right.'

At once they saddled good coursers and set off, riding hard and fast. Each was richly armed, with mailshirt, lance and sharp sword. Three days' unbroken journey brought them to Paris and the high palace.

52

Sir Azemar spoke to the gate-keeper.

'Friend, let us in! We three are messengers from Poitiers.'

'Come in, in God's name!' he said. 'But the warhorses must stay outside.'

Up into the high palace they went and stood together before the king. Gauseran spoke first, for he was old and they wanted ... wise and *a good speaker*, and a good knight *in battle* too.

'God keep and save Roland and Oliver! I bring greeting to all the Twelve Peers in the name of Beton, the good warrior count. He does not greet him whose face gives light, that is to say Charles. May God harass him, for he gave away his sister for silver and shining gold! Fifteen pack animals came to this palace and he gave her in marriage to the traitor Guy, who meant to murder Beton. Instead, he dashed another child against a pillar, a minstrel's son. The God of heaven saved Beton, who now requires this death of you. On Guy, he is avenged; you, he will not forgive. He promises you neither pence nor payments; no, by the Lord who gave us all speech, you shall not see a month pass before he will cause you grief and injury. As long as he can bear arms, you shall not ... for four days.'

The emperor stared at him, then began to laugh and shake his head.

'Friend,' he said, 'you're a very brave man to *come and threaten me* like this! Never ... *

... to love

... to give

... to judge

... knight

... reproach

... command

... accompany

... to carry

... laugh

... assist

* The last 14 lines of the ms are almost completely illegible except for a few words at the ends of the lines.

The lost conclusion of this text may be long or short, see Introduction page 7. A short ending might read as follows:

'Never,' said Charlemagne, 'has anyone ventured to confront me in my own household like this! A brave nephew! Barons, what shall we do with him?'

'Beton's my kinsman and my godson,' said Roland. 'Alive and well, that's excellent news!'

'Well married, too,' said Gauseran. 'His wife is the daughter of a rich and powerful emir.'

'Is she, indeed?' said the king.

'A charming lady,' said Sir Azemar, 'and soon to be a mother.'

'But Beton defies me!' said Charlemagne. 'And he has killed Count Guy, robbed me of my standard-bearer. Who is to lead my armies and go before me in the field?'

'Who but Beton himself?' said Count Oliver. 'Ogier's grandson, son of Duke Bevis, you cannot ask for more.'

'Ride!' said the king. 'Return to Poitiers, tell my sister I acknowledge that I owe her fifteen loads of silver and gold and will pay her when funds allow. Tell my nephew that I do not accept his defiance and now appoint him my standard-bearer. Give him this glove in token. And tell him if the child is a boy, he is to call him Charles!'

Bertrand and his fellows took their leave and returned to Poitiers.

'Come in!' said the gate-keeper. 'Duke Beton has a son, listen to the church bells!'

They entered the high palace and found it full of laughter, joy and merriment. Gauseran gave the emperor's message to Beton and offered him the gold-embroidered glove.

'Take it!' said his mother. 'Take it for the baby's sake.' Beton accepted it and held it out to the baby. It glittered, and the baby gripped it in his fist.

'But he cannot be called Charles,' said Beton, laughing. 'He's baptised already and his name is Daurelet!'

The lady Erimena rocked the baby on her knee, and Daurel the good minstrel took his viol and played a pleasant air to lull the child to sleep.

God send you all health, wealth
and happiness,
and do not forget to be kind to minstrels!

Also published by Llanerch:

GARNIER'S BECKET translated by Janet Shirley

SONG OF ROLAND translated by Janet Shirley

BEOWULF translated by John Porter, and illustrated by Nick Parry

THE MISFORTUNES OF ELPHIN by Thomas Love Peacock (facsimile reprint)

TALIESIN POEMS translated by Meirion Pennar

MAID MARIAN by Thomas Love Peacock (facsimile reprint)

ANGLO-SAXON ELEGIAC VERSE translated by Louis Rodrigues

AN ANGLO-SAXON VERSE MISCELLANY edited and translated by Louis Rodrigues

ANGLO-SAXON RELIGIOUS VERSE ALLEGORIES translated by Louis Rodrigues

CELTIC FOLK TALES FROM ARMORICA by F. M. Luzel, translated by Derek Bryce and illustrated by Anthony Rhys

THE CELTIC LEGEND OF THE BEYOND by Anatole Le Braz, selected translations from *La légende de la mort...* by Derek Bryce, illustrated by Anthony Rhys

BANDAMANNA SAGA translated by John Porter with drawings by Andy Selwood.

For a complete list of c.200 titles, small-press editions and facsimile reprints, write to LLANERCH PUBLISHERS, FELINFACH, LAMPETER, CEREDIGION, WALES, SA48 8PJ.